TheoSophia's

Wisdom School

The Magic of Healing Revealed

THEOSOPHIA ROSE

TheoSophia's Wisdom School
Copyright © 2024 by TheoSophia Rose

ISBN: 979-8895310861(sc)
ISBN: 979-8895310878(e)

All rights reserved. No part of this publication may be reproduced, distributed, or transmitted in any form or by any means, including photocopying, recording, or other electronic or mechanical methods, without the prior written permission of the publisher and/or the author, except in the case of brief quotations embodied in critical reviews and other noncommercial uses permitted by copyright law.

The views expressed in this book are solely those of the author and do not necessarily reflect the views of the publisher, and the publisher hereby disclaims any responsibility for them.

Writers' Branding
(877) 608-6550
www.writersbranding.com
media@writersbranding.com

Advance Praise

"In *TheoSophia's Wisdom School*, TheoSophia Rose has shared her heart and her wisdom, giving readers the tools to discover their gifts and to use them in the world. This insightful book is one you'll read over and over again!"

Matthew Lapp, MS, DC, NSA Practitioner

"TheoSophia Rose's book takes you on the most intimate and powerful journey of the self. Her wisdom demonstrates the incredible power of healing and how it can transform one's life – bringing one to creating and living their destiny. I will be recommending this book highly to friends, colleagues, and clients."

Jessica Baker, LSW, MSW

This book is dedicated to my family: Douglas, Heather, Chance, and David; my teachers, who know who they are; and my wondrous friends. My Light radiates in gratitude to all.

Table of Contents

Advance Praise iii

Introduction vii

Chapter 1: The Desire to Grow 1

Chapter 2: My Story 5

Chapter 3: The Heart Is the Foundation of Healing 11

Chapter 4: Personal Development for the Inquisitive Soul 17

Chapter 5: Advanced Perception 23

Chapter 6: Meditation and Energy Hygiene 31

Chapter 7: Working with Clients 39

Chapter 8: Insight About Working with Chakras
and Their Analysis 45

Chapter 9: How and Why Healing Techniques Change Lives 55

Chapter 10: How to Handle the Obstacles 63

Chapter 11: Embrace the Solution 65

Acknowledgments 67

About the Author 69

Thank You 71

Introduction

"I believe in intuition and inspiration."

Albert Einstein

The number one reason for writing this book is held deep in my heart: it is to help you. I know you have spiritual gifts, and are lost on how to use them. What if you could learn not only what your gifts are, but at the same time learn how you can use them on yourself, and other people? Yes, that's right, the way for you to learn to apply your gifts and understand how to be a healer lies within this book. If I could for a moment take you to the places I've been, the things and people I've seen, the experiences I've had, I know you would love being a Healer of Light, and you would feel driven to reach beyond what you know. Once you are touched with a spark of awareness that you are more than you thought you ever could be, there is no turning back.

Something within you will ignite, you will most likely have chills running all over your body, and right there in that moment, you will want to share that difference with the world. How do I know? I've been there, experienced it myself, and seen it happen for many people.

For over 29 years, I have worked with thousands of people all over the world. After individuals would work with me they would say, "How do you do what you do?" Some asked out of curiosity, others wanted to be able to help people the way I had just helped them. That is how TheoSophia's Wisdom School began. Everyone simply asked me: they wanted more, just like you. Until now the School has been held in person, at times in many cities. Of course, the next question was, "How do you get all your information?" I can say it has been a process.

Healer, Heal Thyself

Well, this is what I did. First, I found a good teacher. With the clarity I developed from a million sessions and a lot of meditation hours, my gifts emerged. I had Divine support from my Higher Self and the Healing Master within me, and together we developed a powerful system of transformation that is constantly changing to be what is needed at the time. It is in constant growth.

Learning to Trust Your Development

I can remember the first validation that my third eye vision was clear. I was in a classroom with others like myself, ready to receive a meditation mantra. The next thing I saw was a beautiful image of a waterfall, and Kuan Yin sitting on a pink lotus. In the Buddhic tradition, Kuan Yin is known as the embodiment of loving kindness and compassion. A few minutes later, I heard my teacher giving us the technique as I had seen it a few minutes before. I knew I was being shown that my vision was very accurate. I learned you must always have validation three times to accept a new truth.

Wisdom Lies Within the Heart

Perhaps you are wondering, why the word wisdom instead of healing. Well, True Wisdom lies within the heart of every soul. As we heal, we begin to move away from seeing the reality of our world from our brain's perception, the ego, which tends to see it in pain and heartache. As we grow spiritually, we energetically bring the brain down into the heart where wisdom lives. This offers us the opportunity to experience love: for self, for others, for Mother and Father God, and to see our reality through the eyes of love. This is very important when you are teaching or working with clients. My last topic for you here is the magic. I believe it can be the most important piece.

The Magic Is God

The path takes you to where you will look at how you feel and believe about a greater source: God. I remember being in Science of Mind class and wondering why I was there.

Knowing God helps you understand that you are Spirit, not the matter of man. Our physical body is simply the vessel our spirit lives within. It is when we begin to believe our thoughts can change our world that we become our truth. So, yes, I sat in that class wondering why I was there, until one day I got it. I surrendered, opened my heart to receive all that God would give me. That was another day I changed. I became more of my true self – knowing that we are creators every day, and that what our lives look like next week depends on what thoughts we are putting out into the world today.

Chapter 1:
The Desire to Grow

"Imagination is more important than knowledge."

Albert Einstein

I would like to introduce you to Noelle, age 42, and a single mother of two children over 20. She worked at the Chamber of Commerce in her town as a bookkeeper. Her older daughter, Sue, had graduated college and was a social worker with the city's social services. Her younger daughter was about to finish her second year of college, working toward becoming a teacher for the primary grades. Noel was very proud of her children and would do anything for them. Often Noel took in extra work for additional income in the evenings. Small businesses often asked her to give lectures about the city.

What most people did not know about Noelle is that she has a great passion for Spirituality. She was raised in a small town in Indiana, and her family went to a Methodist church. She lost her husband years earlier from a car accident and had raised her children by herself. Her life had been all about her children for years. Now that the girls were coming of age and had their own lives, she found time to experience the things she loved to do. For Noel, that was growing spiritually. She often spent some of her spare time on weekends going to spiritual expos. She found that during these journeys, she was learning about Spirit, healing, and angels. Each time, she stretched herself a little further. She had been to a few lectures, and was in awe of some of the things she had seen and experienced.

It was at one of these spiritual expos that she approached me. She saw my banner for TheoSophia's Wisdom School. At first, she seemed shy, yet at the same time curious and full of questions. She sat down, and we began to talk about all the things she had seen at the lectures. She seemed to begin to relax. She told me she felt there was something missing. Something more than what she had heard so far that made it all work. She wanted to know how people got to a point where they could help people. She felt there had to be something in between opening inside and becoming a person who does the work on someone else. I understood everything she was telling me, and I asked her to tell me more. I could tell she had more to share. She shared with me that she wanted to talk about something that was bothering her. I touched her hand lightly and told her sure, I was there for her.

On one evening when she had stayed late at the Chamber of Commerce, her thoughts were on an Angel evening she was going to the next weekend. She found herself saying a prayer for someone to bring her answers about her spiritual experiences. No sooner did the thought leave her mind than a pile of papers swooshed across the room and landed on the floor. Yet there was no one around. She admitted it frightened her a little, but most of all, she found she was frustrated with herself for not knowing more.

It was clear to me she felt the presence of the Angels that she was talking to in the room. It was also becoming clear to me that her real problem was having spiritual gifts yet not knowing how to apply them. It was keeping her walking between two worlds.

As I listened, she became more comfortable, and we continued to talk. She told me about when her younger daughter was getting ready to go to college and trying to decide whether to stay at home and go to Purdue University, or go west to UCLA in California. I could see that Noelle was getting teary eyed as she thought of the memory. The west coast was so far away.

During this time, she often wanted to plead with her daughter to stay home, yet she found her mouth would remain silent, as she kept hearing a message inside her head: *You have raised her well. Trust in her, she will make the best choice.*

Every time she heard these words, she got chills all over. In the end, her daughter chose to go the state college near home, but it was clearly her own choice. Noelle was relieved not just because her daughter was staying home, but also because she felt no regrets. She had not guilted her daughter into staying home. Together, we took a cleansing breath and just looked at each other. I could feel she was waiting for me to say something that would give her peace, something that would make it all real.

I felt Noelle desired to resolve this problem about her gifts, yet felt afraid. Ever since her husband had left, long ago, the girls had become her life. She wasn't sure how to contemplate her life alone. As I listened, I decided to talk to her more.

I asked Noelle, if we find your gifts are real, what would that do for you? Her response was that first, it would let her know she wasn't crazy. She would want to know more so she could understand what was really happening, and she would want to learn to do it correctly. Most importantly, with the girls growing up and living their own lives, she would have the opportunity to not only focus more on herself, but to help people. She would have a passion within her heart that would be fulfilled. I could feel it coming from her heart, a deep compassion. She was crying.

I told Noelle I thought she was experiencing the beginning of her gifts emerging. Her energy field was increasing from all the various events she had participated in and an awakening was happening. I told her that my book – this book, *TheoSophia's Wisdom School* – would be a guide to help her to know the love within herself, supporting her in becoming a friend to herself. Most of all, this book would take her on a journey of the discovery of healing. Certainly, it would tell her about gifts and about how a greater Light allows them to unveil, about the world, about disease, and how to begin to understand the process and the power of thought. Lastly, reading the case studies would show her the power of God's Light moving through a clear vessel. All this would give Noelle the opportunity to study, prepare, and embrace her gifts, doing all that is necessary to allow them to unveil and to allow her to begin to live with sacred honor and respect, so that she could begin to do what she loves to do, which is to help people.

And so it will be for you.

Your answers lie right here in this book. *TheoSophia's Wisdom School* is going to show you the way. You will understand not only how to develop your gifts, but also gain insight about how healing and energy work, offering you the opportunity to help others.

In the following chapters, we'll explore:

- Heart as the Foundation of Healing
- Personal Development for the Inquisitive Soul
- Advanced Perception
- Meditation & Energy Hygiene
- Working with Clients
- Insight About Working with Chakras & Their Analysis
- How & Why Healing Techniques Change Lives
- How to Handle the Obstacles
- Living the Dream

Chapter 2:
My Story

"Go confidently in the direction of your dreams and live the life you have imagined."

Henry David Thoreau

I want to take you to a small town in Indiana. I lived with my parents and two brothers on a 200-acre farm. As I look back now, it was a wonderful experience. Let me tell you about the magical part. My father was the seventh son of 12 children. It is said that great gifts are given to the seventh son of a family. Well, for sure my dad was very gifted. I have strong memories of him sitting us down at the table, where he would see the future with the use of horoscope cards. I have never seen these cards anywhere else. In the magic of the moment, he could make them move above the table, in the air. He did not do it for outsiders, mostly just the family. So, the truth about my early life is that I lived and believed in magic. Not the kind of magic people do in shows today, I mean the magic that is from the powerful energy of Source.

I remember going for long walks up to the pond on the farm. I had little friends, fairies and other tiny beings that would come and spend the day with me. Three of them would come back to my bedroom with me: a pirate, a knight in shining armor, and a damsel. They stayed in my hope chest until I would get home from school. There were times at the pond when I would look up and see a shack, the energy would call out to me to come in. Inside it looked very sparse, a simple table and chairs. When I sat down I looked across from me and there was Jesus. We would sit and talk and take walks. There were times a large balloon would come and we would ride up into heaven. We would walk down a corridor of the soul, seeing picture after picture of me in other lifetimes. At the time, I did not think this was odd or weird. Yes, I did talk to everyone and everything: the animals, the birds, etc. This was the vivid capacity of the third-eye vision I had come into this world with. Once I became a young woman, I seemed to only focus on boys – I'm sure you know the feeling. So, as years went on, I forgot all about my gifts and the magical life I had lived Then, when I was getting close to 31 years old, I started to have car accidents. Two of them were on my birthday, exactly one year apart. I ended up having a total of five car accidents, and experienced a lot of pain.

I was going to the chiropractor every day for the physical pain; I wore a shoulder brace and hip support. I was a mess, but the driven part of me would not allow me to miss a day of work. So, for six days a week, I went and sat on a stool, of all things, and did my job. One Monday, my chiropractor told me I should go to see her mother. She shared with me that her mother was a *special person* who did a different kind of work that helped people change their lives. So, you know, I made an appointment, where I met a nice woman named June. During the appointment, I was lying there on a table in her living room just letting her do her healing technique on me: muscle testing to release emotional pain. In the next moment, I almost jumped out of my skin. There was a loud *boom*!!! June had a large stack of books on a chair, and one had fallen onto the floor from the middle of the stack. Wow, that startled me. Then I heard her say, "This must be for you."

I was beginning to think she was very weird. She handed me the book, and I saw that the title was *Opening to Channeling*. I did not know what that meant, and I really wasn't sure what was happening. She said to take the book home, give it a good read, and see what would happen. Oh, and by the way, I did feel better after my session. I felt so uplifted and free of pain that I knew in that minute that *I wanted to help others*, just like June had helped me. I had been living that pain for so long, and now I saw a light at the end of the tunnel.

You'll never guess what happened next. I went home, and had about an hour before I had to make dinner, so I opened the book and started to read. It told me to sit quietly and how to bring in the light and my Higher Self. Hmmmm. Then it happened: I heard a beautiful voice, a man's voice, calling me and speaking to me: *Little one. I am here now*.

I will never forget that moment. Everything began to flood back into my awareness. The farm, the pond, my father, my spirit friends, the shack where I met Jesus, the air balloon we would ride up to heaven. They were all there again, right inside of me, loving me.

I called June. She didn't seem surprised, and offered to call someone named Eleanor who helped people in these situations. So yes, it was the beginning of the journey of my soul, one I am still walking today. Eleanor told me that at the ages of 7-11 years old, we choose whether to remember our growth and development from our earlier years, even from our past lives. If you don't choose to remember, the third eye closes. Well, mine was reopening very quickly. I mention this because you need to understand that this could be true for you also. You had great third eye vision at one time, and if not when you were younger, then perhaps in another lifetime. Eleanor also told me that this was a new beginning in my life, and not to be afraid, that it would feel familiar. I learned to trust these people who seemed to know what they were talking about. Everyone is given the gifts of the universe. It depends on the journey they have walked as to the level of development they experience.

So here I was with gifts and the question: Where do I go from here? I began listening to my inner voices and learning about Spirit – about myself, really. I found a teacher. I learned the technique June had offered to me. I became certified, and I felt very natural doing it. I began to see visions for my clients. My next challenge came when the creators of One Brain – the technique I had just learned – announced that individuals were not allowed to see visions or channel for clients. I began to follow my intuition and found a good teacher. I had one to two sessions a week to heal myself and old issues. The clearer I got, the clearer my experience with my inner teachers became. I began to work on surrendering and listening to my Healing Master for what was next. During this time, I developed new modalities of Light work that are still used today.

I want to share with you one of the most powerful experiences of my spiritual life. I had begun to feel the desire inside to be a minister. A powerful place within me was developing, and I wanted to speak with my Teacher, yet once again, even with all I had done, I needed validation outside of myself. I was insecure. At a seminar doing the subconscious work, I had met a man named Douglas. He told me he was going on a trip to Thailand to learn to meditate and that everyone who went became a minister. Yes, you're right, as soon as he said it, I was going, I had to go. My husband was very against it, yet my heart knew I was being called. Over the next few months before I went, my husband told me he knew I would never come home, over and over again. While I thought at the time he was being silly, his vision was accurate. I did not return home the person who left. It still gives me the chills to think of it.

Off to Thailand I went, all 27 hours of flying. I was so excited, I didn't care how long it took. We traveled through Seoul, Korea and Bangkok, Thailand, and upon arrival in Chiang Mai, I met my Teacher. I still call him that. He will always be my Teacher in my heart. This journey became more than becoming a minister, it was about surrender, faith, healing, the heart, believing, and, put simply, embracing my soul. His words would vibrate through me when he spoke. We went and did and saw so many things. I will pick a few life changers and share them with you.

At one of our meetings, my Teacher told us he knew about a child Buddha that lived close to where we were staying. At the time, he was only eight years old. He lived in a village where a highly-thought-of monk lived called the Black Monkey. He had three gifts: the ability to fly, the ability to heal from the heart, and invisibility. Before he was to leave the Earth, he was instructed to give his gifts to young Buddhas. There were three boys, each of whom received one of his gifts. The time was set when we were going to get to meet the young Buddha who received the gift of healing from the heart. The night before this event while we were out at the night market, I tripped and fell. My ankle turned all black, and I could hardly walk on it. But you are probably getting to know me. I hobbled my way to see the little Buddha the next morning.

When we arrived, we sat on a blue tarp with lots of flowers all around. We were told we could ask the Buddha for a healing. I sat for a while just breathing in my experience of where I was, and what was happening. I was going to meet a Buddha. I thought a painful black foot would be the perfect thing to get healed. I waited for my turn, and then the time came. I explained how I had fallen and hurt my foot, it was all black. The interpreter was speaking with him as he was looking at me, and then she said, "He is sorry, but Buddhas cannot touch the feet of any soul."

The joy and anticipation within me collapsed. I sat there holding back the tears, trying very hard not to be a baby. I just wanted to run, but I couldn't even get up without everybody seeing me and disrupting the gathering. Then I felt something happening. My black foot was tingling. I nudged my friend so I could be sure I wasn't imagining it. We could see the black on my ankle moving, going into the ground, just like ants. Yes, you heard me. It was a miracle. I looked up, and saw the Buddha sitting there, smiling at me. He had not touched my foot. I realized he had healed me from his heart, his treasured gift. I sat there in amazement: What had just happened? I will never forget it. That day, my faith began to run strong and pure like a river. At the end of the gathering, I got up and walked away. Everyone was talking about how my foot was fine, like nothing had ever happened to it. I knew in that moment that not only was I meant to be there to know a deeper faith in God, I was there to meet this young Buddha and to experience the depth of healing and transformation that heart healing had brought to me.

I realized more deeply than ever before that we are all given gifts. It is up to us to discover when and how to take that first step into a new world, embrace our gifts, and bring them into clarity. I have spent the last 28 years helping others. I believe anyone can be successful on this journey.

In truth, you and I are not different at all. It's about taking one step at a time and getting excited about where the journey might take you, knowing the soul – which is responsive to your blueprint – knows exactly where you are and where you are going. I could never have told you at the beginning of my journey where I would end up. I'm not sure I'm there yet. But I can tell you that I wouldn't want to have missed a moment. I love myself so deeply that today, I understand who I am. And that's a gift I will always cherish.

Chapter 3:
The Heart Is the Foundation of Healing

*"Few are those who see with their own eyes and
feel with their own hearts."*

Albert Einstein

Learning How the Heart Heals

Your heart is the most powerful part of your being. Perhaps you think I am speaking of your physical heart. I am not. You have an energetic spiritual heart. It is one of your chakras, which we will discuss later. For now, allow me to bring you awareness of your spiritual heart. When you first came to life, the union of your mother's and father's cells started your cell growth, generating your heart. Just imagine: Later in your life, when you experience the movement of Ascension, you will also be moving through your heart. As you contemplate this for a moment, imagine the power of the magical energy your heart is! It is your movement of beginning, and the movement of leaving life as we know it. If we ask why, the answer is simple: Mother Father God resides in your heart. Before you came to Earth to live as a human, you, as every individual has, sat with Mother Mary to create your heart. So, as you can touch your heart in this moment, know some very powerful beings have been there, and still live within you today. I believe this speaks to the love they hold for you. Your destiny in this life is to become aware of how lovable you are, to choose to love all of you, and to radiate that love.

Self-love, relationship to self, and acceptance are the main components of healing. Healer, heal thyself.

A lot of books have been written on the subject of self-love. Over the years I have worked with people, I have learned that patterns of consciousness move through the universe like a river. We are without a doubt all a part of the oneness. We all have the same patterns. Mine may show up differently than yours, but I assure you they are there. How do I know this? Let me show you by telling you about a typical week in my practice.

Perhaps my first client of the week would want help on loving herself. By the end of the week, over half the people I worked with would have also come in with self-love as an issue. I would notice the pattern, and so the level of clearing would get deeper. At my school, we acknowledge and work with an understanding of soul groups: groups of likeminded individuals who come together in order to grow together. Even if there are times that they have no contact with each other, they end up experiencing similar patterns in their lives. If you expand this idea to, say, all of America, it's not so farfetched to think that patterns are being expressed and released through soul groups at the same time, all over the world. Very interesting.

So, let's get back to self-love. Are you one of those people that like to do and give to everybody? If you are, consider: What is the last thing you did for yourself? Did you get a massage, buy flowers, have a special dinner, buy a new outfit? This is how we begin to look at self-love. Next, think about what you like about yourself, and then what you don't like about you. Which list is longer? Are you able to accept that you are a spiritual being?

Did you know you can only love another to the extent that you love yourself? This is difficult sometimes for people to understand. Contemplate with me here for a moment: How could you give more love? Self-love is fed every time there is a healing, a release, a change of perception. Neither you nor I can know in this moment what the greatest love feels like because we are still growing. In fact, our growth never ends.

Self-acceptance lies in the chakra at the back of your throat. It allows confidence and success to flourish. Many times, we reject ourselves for the simplest reasons. Often, rejection originates with how you were raised, how you were supported, or even if you could use crayons when you were little. All these reasons, and many, many more.

My client Mary, age 38, was not allowed to use crayons and paints, to play in the mud, or to be out in the rain when she was little. We were trying to understand why she had no interest in being creative. Her mother had been a perfectionist – need I say more? To deal with this issue, Mary and I worked together to heal her inner child of the anger and fear of messing something up. The client agreed to be the new mom to the inner child, and to give her child permission to be creative. Acceptance is powerful work and can be very rewarding.

Love, in a relationship, is to be shared, not controlled. You live in a time today when there are many divorces and many disgruntled relationships. Relationship work is also very rewarding and at times very deep. Without being aware, you have most likely been taught to love by giving your love to another. Most vows confirm this. In truth, it is about becoming the love you are. Become a strong, independent, courageous, spirit of light, and feel comfortable in your own body. When you achieve this, you will then magnetize a being of like development to you. Together, you can share your love as it springs from the powerful self-love you each have discovered within. When we give our love to another, we have no control of it any longer.

Discovering self-love and then sharing it with another prevents you from becoming vulnerable to being hurt. We could acknowledge this as an unhealthy attachment. As you grow upon your path, you will find that you are the love you have been looking for.

The Ocean of God in the Heart

One of the first patterns you might consider healing is the feeling of being alone. Know that this idea of aloneness is simply a human thought. In your life as a human, situations may have shown up where you believed there was no one there for you. I invite you to become aware that patterns like this one come into your life not only for you to become clearer, but to guide you toward your truth. The classroom of Earth is set up to help you grow. You began with loving parents, grandparents, friends, etc., until the first time someone was not there for you. At about the age of seven, you were no longer in the aura of your mother, and the world felt and looked different. You began to have feelings of being hurt, afraid, angry, and lonely, to name a few.

Your choices, decisions, feelings, and failures all play a part in your life. It is how you become you. Yet, as you quickly discovered, the journey continues, despite the chaos that can be happening. Everything begins to build upon itself. When you become aware that all the labels that are defining you – mother, sister, daughter, friend, employee – are illusions, you may decide, like myself, to enlist someone to help you sort things out. Within your heart, there is always an answer. Why? Because Mother Father God live there.

How does it make you feel to walk along a beach? Uplifted, safe, at peace? Yes, I would agree. Well, if you were to imagine that you would walk into the front of your heart chakra, know that you would find an ocean of God, complete with a beach and shining sun, warm water, and a chair just for you, if you would like. If you want some company on your walk, just ask.

Any being of light would come to you. Everything you have ever felt you emotionally needed from outside can be found there in your heart. Yes, it is a process of developing faith, belief, and surrender.

Faith, Belief, and Surrender

Faith is something that will continue to grow and get stronger every moment you walk your path. There are conflicting thoughts about faith, much like the dogma of a religion. Here, I am speaking about faith as the relationship between you and God. As we grow, and especially as we are learning about our gifts and helping others, we learn to love. Places where we thought we weren't enough, or where we thought we did something wrong, begin to change. We begin to see that we have courage, that we are strong. We understand that we are love.

As you touch your soul and discover you are more than you thought you were, you realize you are becoming spirit instead of simply the limited experience of humanity. As a spiritual being, you will begin to desire to fulfill your yearning to belong. In this place, you will begin to know you are not alone, that you are surrounded by many beings of light within you and without. Your head, heart, and hand will reach out to God to walk with you every step of the way. When you cannot walk, He will always carry you.

Terry, age 43, has studied with me for a while, and was working on two things specifically: She was unhappy in her marriage, and she felt that she did not make enough money to pay her bills. She would sit and get frustrated trying to figure a way out. She had panic attacks. When she called me, I listened. I knew her, and knew she was aware of God. Yet, as I listened, I didn't hear conversation about God. She was angry and blaming it on everyone and everything else.

I always say that when there is an emotional response, the answer lies within you. So, Terry and I talked, and I asked her to look inside at what she was angry about. And there it was. She felt God wasn't there for her. Well, I'll tell you as I told her, that isn't the God I know. The realization that she could change her life by deepening her belief system and changing her perception was amazing to her. Without going into all the details, let me share with you what Terry's success is today. She brought God into her work as her Partner, and into her home and finances. She surrendered to whatever outcome was the highest and best for her. Terry received a promotion at her job with a higher salary. She met a new man, an old friend from high school who had just thought to call her, and they fell in love. When she told her husband about him, her husband had met someone else, also. They filed for divorce. That's not all. Recently, she sold her house where they had lived, in one day, and she and her daughter moved into a new townhome. Really, you can't make this up. Putting God in action is such a powerful experience. It flows through the heart out into the world. The only thing you must to do is surrender to the outcome and believe.

Empathy vs. Sympathy

I have found that many people who have gifts, who feel they are empathic, take on everyone else's stuff. Perhaps this is true for you. It might help to clarify things by understanding that sympathy comes from the feelings we have for another person when we think they need help or are suffering. Empathy, on the other hand, is a place where you can simply sit in compassion and see individuals in their strength. Love them for where they are. Now, this can certainly be challenging without training. Unless you learn how to master your gifts, you can't know how to set boundaries, how to work with your caretaker cord – or even what that is – or understand the need to get a grip on your own energy field.

Together, you and I have journeyed through the heart. We have made a few stops and learned a few things. Know that the greatest healer is love. The work on the heart will never end. It does not have to be seen as a chore, but rather as a walk across a beautiful and colorful bridge of personal development. To have a desire to help others is to say, "I am ready to help myself discover love: my love, and my relationship with God." It truly is a matter of "healer, heal thyself."

What's next is more understanding about developing your gifts, how to grow and undertake the necessary work to be done. My invitation to you is to become aware of the magical action your gifts hold, own those gifts, and help others in the world by surrendering your heart and allowing your gifts to bloom. This will make a difference in the world, and in your life.

Chapter 4: Personal Development for the Inquisitive Soul

"In the middle of difficulty lies opportunity."

Albert Einstein

Thoughts Are Things

I want to share some interesting facts you might not know. Let's begin with the awareness that *thoughts are things*. Imagine a little person, an inch tall. Dress it up and send it out to the universe. It will come back to you with a million little people just like itself. In other words, when you think a thought like happiness, very quickly you will feel a greater happiness from the action of the thought. If you are angry and this thought goes out and brings back more anger, well, it's not so good.

God has given all souls the power of creation. We also received the gift of free will. Every day, all day long, you are creating your world from what you think. Most people do not even have the awareness that it is happening. So, imagine that what you think today is what you create in your world next week. On the path of helping others, it is important to do some personal housecleaning and become aware of how are you creating your world. Have your thoughts become more purposeful?

Energy Follows Thought

Fact number two: Energy follows thought. It is a universal hermetic law. This truth is one you'll also use every day, especially when you work with your gifts and energy. Let's imagine you desire to send loving energy to your knee. Upon thinking the thought, "I call in the pink light of love to embrace the cells of my knee," the action will occur. There is no doubt. "Energy follows thought" is a law of the universe. It is so in your everyday life, and particularly in your life as you become a healer.

I will give you another for instance. Perhaps you have a thought about your friend John. Upon thinking it, the thought arrives to John, and he thinks of you. Have you ever had someone say, "I was just thinking of you"? It is often considered to be intuition. Some people will see the face of the sender. Some will have a sense or feeling. Simply put, you are what you think. The more you can put positive thoughts into your consciousness, the more you will reveal the real you. In the same instance, the more you can observe yourself and your thinking, the more you will begin to understand why your life looks like it does.

What Is Disease?

Disease is a dysfunctional thought. All disease is a result of a thought gone bad. Once a dysfunctional thought is released into consciousness, it takes form as rejection, anger, loss, hurt, and so on as your life moves through situations day to day. Next, this thought continues to move through the fields of energy of your aura. If it is not stopped, examined by you, and embraced with your love, this thought will eventually reach the physical body and create a disease.

If you think of all the thoughts you have released in a lifetime, you'll see that many have become patterns, and patterns have greater strength. This is the reason to be on the path of personal development. I believe all things can be healed – they are simply thoughts that need transformation. The power of thought comes into your life when you understand it has the capacity to create and to transform – that, basically, it is alive.

You have probably heard of *affirmations*. At the beginning of my path, I said "I am love" about a million times a day. Why would I do that? I made a choice. I was taking the power of my thought back. I no longer wanted random thoughts to be the cause of trauma in my life. My intentional thought offered me the opportunity to know more love and to begin to discover it within myself.

Another practice I carried out was to write, ten times a day, a statement of something I wanted to bring into my life. I found this to be very productive. I suggest you consider doing something like this for yourself. It could be any affirmation, but I like the one about love. Try saying it as many times a day as you can, because it is the place to begin. Now, we are making it a reality in your life.

Another interesting action is to create an affirmation of drawing unexpected income to yourself. I suggest giving this a try. You must keep in mind not to spend time on thoughts trying to imagine where it will come from. This is many lessons all in one. Learning to surrender, to release and let go, and to be willing to be disciplined.

The Sushumna, Your Channel of Light

The Sushumna is the central channel of light that exists vertically within the center of the body, traveling the full length of the middle of the spinal cord. The light – pranic energy – enters this channel at the top of the crown chakra and at the root chakra. It can begin with being only a ¼-inch in width, and increase to extend beyond the universe, many miles wide, through personal development. This channel is known as the pathway to enlightenment, the pathway through which energy rises on its way to affirm ascension. If we look at the seven-chakra human system, the chakras are connected and rooted into the Sushumna. This is how prana moves into the system and out through the chakras, generating wellbeing.

The Importance of Grounding and Living in the Present

This subject is a necessity. You may have gifts, but unless you can increase what we call your light quotient, which is how much light your body can hold, there will be no magic to make them happen. In school, I tell my students that when the day comes that one of them walks into the room and I can not only see their aura, but feel it, then that is the day that person will be grounded enough. So, here is what you can do. Place your hands palms up. Recite these words from your heart: "I am connecting to the crystalline grid of Mother Earth." Imagine dropping a little anchor from above your head to down inside the tube of the Sushumna. Let it fall, down deep into the center of the Earth. As it falls downward, you will begin to feel Mother Earth's response, feeling either a tingling in your hands, or possibly heat. Your light is increased. Now the next issue is learning to hold that light. You will be able to in time; it doesn't always happen in a day. Keep practicing.

When people have a lot of headaches, it can be from not being down inside their body. Other possibilities are dizziness, confusion, panic attacks, tremendous fear, etc. There are great rewards for you to walk in the world and be deeply grounded. Some of them are to feel strong, confident, secure, and present.

Ego/Personality

Everyone has an ego. I will give you some information so you are equipped to find and become aware of yours. The ego is the same energy as your personality, and is located within the four lower chakras. Chakras 5 through 7 are higher chakras, not usually affected and controlled by ego, but still capable of holding patterns that need healing. Ego acts out in many ways. Do you ever hear a small voice telling you perhaps to not listen to something? Or find that you are controlling at times, always wanting things to be your way? Manipulation, betrayal, having a chip on the shoulder, and anger are all things the ego is trying to tell you are necessary to survive. This is not so.

Imagine that you are on a large sailboat in the ocean. The ego has the tiller. You want to go to the beach, but the ego decides you need to go to work. It's possible that you will find yourself sailing off to work and being satisfied about it, feeling that you have no choice in the matter. Personal development is about discovering the voice of your ego, choosing to take back control of your life and no longer give your ego power. With respect to healing, I will give you some insight about how taking your power back can change not only your energy, but your life.

Let's go to your second chakra for a moment. The front of this chakra concerns your emotions and connections to outer relationships. Perhaps you will agree with me that this area can feel like a roller coaster ride. A lot of energy movement is sometimes lost here. Now, if instead, this chakra had already released the power of the ego, you could choose to heal the patterns that are connected to emotions and relationships, and there would be a change. When this chakra has reached a level of clarity, it will, like all the four lower chakras, shift consciousness up into a higher realm. The second chakra will become creative. The entire energy of this chakra goes from an orange to a rainbow of colors, ready to receive ideas and to become a creator. Something like an artist's palette.

The Other Side – Divinity

The choice, once the ego has been quieted, is to experience your divinity. There is no letting go of the ego, it is a part of us. You can quiet the voice, freeing you to make different choices. You do this by consciously placing the ego within your heart every day, giving it a new job to do other things instead of running your life. You will find that your mind will become quieter, and you will begin to discover your true self.

The first part of your divinity that you will come in contact with is the Higher Self. It is waiting above you to come down over your energy field and offer you transformation. It is basically an energetic copy of yourself, but has no patterns and is of your divinity. It has chakras that are clear. As you begin to grow, the Higher Self reaches for you, resulting in the melding together of the first two chakras and enhancing your transformation. It does not happen quickly; it is a process. For instance, the divine root chakra of the Higher Self will come down over the crown of your humanness. This action will begin to allow the divinity and knowing of your human field to be showered with light from the Higher Self's root chakra. This is going to bring you to a place of feeling differently about Mother Father God, closer in contact and feeling, finding a greater foundation within Mother Father God. As this process continues, you will discover more issues will emerge, a deeper growth will occur, and finally you will become your Higher Self in form.

Next, we will begin to look at what else the Higher Self has in mind for you as we continue the journey of personal development to unveil your gifts, reveal your dream come true of helping others, and of loving the work you do.

Chapter 5:
Advanced Perception

"The only real valuable thing is intuition."

Albert Einstein

Unveiling Your Gifts Is All About Perception

The next piece to unveiling your gifts is all about your perception. The higher chakras I mentioned earlier become the doorways to many gifts. The throat chakra, for instance, offers you the expression not only of your thoughts, but eventually of divine thoughts expressed through your voice. If you are fascinated by healing with your voice, this will be a chakra of great interest. You will learn all about frequencies and how to dissolve a negative pattern with sound. Not only will you express frequencies, but you will learn to hear them. One day, you will know how people are feeling simply by hearing their voice.

Connecting to Your Higher Self

Within the realm of the healing arts, there is a great controversy on this next subject. I am going to share with you the path that offers the greatest clarity. You will create an experience where you will have no doubt about where your information is coming from. This is the piece that could be bringing you the most discomfort about finding your gifts and helping other people. With dedication, I will help you change all that. You must do the work. Not everyone just sits down and finds that everything comes to them right away. Everyone is different.

I have explained to you who the Higher Self is: your first level of divinity. Yes, as I explained, there will be a process of it slowly coming down and "over lighting" you, as it is called. Slowly, as patterns are released and more of the chakras meld, you will become clearer. As you work with the Higher Self, you will be able to sense it, feel the energy, and, most importantly, be able to hear it.

Why would you desire this? When you are working with individuals, you want to put the ego aside, and merge with your divinity to receive and share the highest and best information for them. This practice will take some time and dedication, yet it will be so rewarding. We are now talking about your inner relationship, which consists of you and your divinity. This will undoubtedly become your greatest evolution and deepest work. I may have mentioned it earlier; I will mention it here again. How can you help another until you begin the path of healing yourself? Healer, heal yourself. Here, I suggest that you have a mentor or healer work with you to release your patterns. There are those who believe they can heal themselves. It is not true. That little best friend we all have called the ego does not allow it.

Automatic Writing

A question I often get is, "What would I say to my Higher Self?" Well, dear ones, whatever you would want to ask, the universe is your canvas. I suggest starting with automatic writing.

Automatic writing is sitting in a surrendered state and asking your Higher Self to come and sit within you. You are going to choose to allow the Higher Self to write through your hand, moving the pen, allowing it to write. Simply begin to make circles with your pen on the paper. It gives the movement energy so that the Higher Self can respond to your question. Our Higher Selves usually write a lot larger than our writing normally is. Ask a question, and allow yourself to be quiet and receive. After three days, go back and look at what you have written, and you will know if your ego wrote it or if your Higher Self did. This will help you learn the feeling and frequency of your Higher Self while at the same time building trust. I often have individuals tell me, "Oh, I already do readings." But when I then ask where their information comes from, no one ever knows. So, trust me, taking the time to develop the gift of perception is well worth it down the road.

My client, Susan, had been studying and working on her path for a while. I like to call it taking a vacation on the path. She was not living her journey every day, but only on days she wanted to. One day, she called to tell me that she had had a powerful experience, and all these wonderful things were going to happen. She was told she had a large mission because she was so powerful. I knew right away what had happened. Susan was one who did not really like to do her meditations or practices. This is a way the ego gets in the way, as I was talking about.

Understand that the greatest mission on Earth right now is to discover the love you are and radiate it to the world. God is simple. When someone talks about their big mission, it is their ego talking. I encourage you to do the work; the work always works. Susan's situation ended well; she finally got it. Her discernment has become clear, along with her path. She wonders what took her so long to get involved.

Perception through the eyes of the ego will always be skewed. It will tell you to blame someone else, to be the poor me, or to do something like walk away. These things create victimization. You want to become empowered, in light, in life, and in love. Seeing through the eyes of love will always show you an answer you may not have found otherwise. Remember, in God there are a million possibilities. You must not try to figure it out. When you surrender and allow, the truth will be brought to you.

Inner Signal

Another great gift we have been given is called the Inner Signal. This is an intuitive response to a question. It can be a movement of the head from right to left or forward and backward, seeing an image, or movement of an arm or hand. Again, you would want to work with this until you have developed a trust in its accuracy. The mantra *ham sa* is used to increase clarity and inner alignment during this training process.

Receiving Impressions

So, we have talked about connecting to your Higher Self and the Inner Signal, now let's look at receiving impressions. When you are sitting waiting to receive a message from spirit, whether it is your Higher Self or an angel, we call that receiving an impression. The light energy of spirit is sending an impression of some kind to you to share information. This could be an image, a sense of an image, a feeling in your heart, or a feeling somewhere else in your body.

You could even feel cold or hot. Through practice, you will begin to decipher the messages and how to interpret them. If you feel like you can't sense anything, then do what everyone else does: Simply imagine. Imagination is 99% accurate. It is the fastest way to support your perception to grow. Let's see if you understand what I mean. Can you imagine an old-fashioned rocking chair moving back and forth? Ok, now imagine you are sitting in the rocker. Are you able to sense the movement – do you feel calm? Are you able to make the old rocker change into a red couch? Why not take a moment, and sit and see if it is soft? Can you change it to blue? Well, wonderful then, you will do just fine.

In spiritual development, the words "I can't" are never spoken. We must remember our teaching about thought. If we believe we can't, we will create that we can't and be our own worst enemy. My answer is practice, practice, practice. Did you know you can do anything you can put your mind to? It's true. The energy will follow the thought and create it. This means that life as you know it will change. It is all about perception. You want to dream big.

Heightening Kinesthetic Ability

Perhaps you are asking yourself, what is kinesthetic ability? It is the sensory perception of movement and a greater awareness of one's own body. Let me see if I can help show you what part it plays in becoming a practitioner of healing. This gift comes from within the root chakra. It is about feeling energy, muscles, and, for some, feeling inside of the body. It is a wonderful gift when someone is in physical pain and you can go to the pain and receive the impression from either the muscle or the wound to be able to help them let go of the pain. Having this gift by no means says you are taking the pain on for them. No, you will learn how the energy of God touches and transforms the illusion. Learning the correct way to use and develop this gift is so powerful. There was a man named Das Kalos in Greece. He could touch a broken arm and heal it in two minutes. Now that is some level of concentration and higher light! This could be you someday.

The Gift of Running Light Energy in Multiple Ways

I'm sure you are aware of running energy through the hands. The key word here is going to be "control." As you develop and begin to become clearer, you will most likely have a desire to deepen your gift. Running energy through the hands is still done by Reiki healers and those who use the palms of the hands. I'm going to simply present you with other possibilities and allow you to contemplate them.

First, we take one finger and imagine that the very top end of the finger is the crown of a body, and the fingertip pad corresponds to the third eye. So, in truth, you have a third eye on every finger. Not only can you send light through the fingertips, you can see, feel, and receive impressions. Using the fingertips in some situations creates an intense focus and a greater ability to serve your client. As you develop, there will also be possibilities of using your eyes and heart. Perhaps you are ahead of me and understand, and you are right, that you can offer healing to someone just by offering energy through your finger. Let's say someone has nausea in their belly. You can go to any finger on the middle crease, offer healing light, and they will feel relief. This is from the understanding of holographic healing, which we will talk about more in a few chapters.

The Magic and Levels of the Energy Field: How Does It Work?

Let's go over some basics about your aura. First, we all have one. Everyone's aura is uniquely different. What you may not know, is that there are levels of understanding in the aura, and each level is connected to a chakra. I will go into a detailed description of the chakra characteristics in a later chapter. For now, I will tell you the function of the chakras and why they are important.

Chakra is a Sanskrit word meaning wheel. They were named so because of the circular shape to the spinning energy centers which exist in our subtle etheric body, the non-matter energetic counterpart to our physical body, which is made of matter. There are seven major chakras which are located along the spine, reaching in front of and behind the body. Each chakra is connected to a certain part of the body, system, and organ. The chakra takes in energy and moves it through, by the means of spinning, to transform that energy into light that can be used by the body to bring balance and healing. The amount of flow and lifeforce moving through the chakra depends on the spin, the width of the spin, the velocity, and finally, the clarity. Within the chakras are tiny streams of light called nadis. This is to the energy field like the nervous system is to the body. That which you thought was simple, is very complex. Intuitive individuals all see the impression of the chakras differently. I happen to see them as flowers. I learn a lot from the condition of the petals when I am healing an individual. Perhaps you can begin to see why it is powerful to use the fingers with their greater focus than the palm of the hand.

The Levels of the Auric Field: 1-7

Getting back to what I wanted to share with you. The human aura consists of seven levels of etheric energy. Each level of the aura is connected to a chakra and moves out around the body, creating a large, egg-shaped field of light. Each level of the field has an effect on the behavior and well-being of the human within the aura. All the levels of light, along with the chakras they are aligned to, connect to the Sushumna, bringing it all together.

Level 1: Etheric Body

Connected to the root chakra, and extending 360 degrees from 1 to 3 inches around the body. The color can be dark blue, gray, or brown, depending on the physical health of the individual. The deeper the hue of blue, the healthier the individual is. This is an etheric blueprint of your physical body. The growth of tissue cells is here.

Level 2: Emotional

Connected to the second, sacral chakra, and made up of light pink and light blue. This level is connected to the etheric level extending out from the body. It shows our feelings and emotions. If you are unhappy, it will show up, literally, as a dark cloud in this field.

Level 3: Mental

Connected to the third chakra, known as the solar plexus, and extending to the emotional field out from the body. It is a yellow field of light, and is full of mental thoughts. The more thoughts you have, the darker and denser this field is. I often see this field in people as appearing like many cars in a traffic jam. This tells me their mind is like a monkey mind, in constant motion.

Level 4: Astral

Connected to the fourth, or heart, chakra, it is an emerald green, and speaks to our unconditional love for others. This level is connected to the mental field extending out from the body up to two feet.

Level 5: Creative Expression

Connected to the fifth, or throat, chakra, it is blue, with the hue dependent upon level of development. It speaks to our soul's mission. This level is connected to the astral field.

Level 6: Celestial

Connected to the sixth, or third eye chakra, this level is related to the angelic realm, and unconditional love for all creation. Light blue or purple, this level is connected to creative expression.

Level 7: Knowingness

Connected to the seventh, or Crown chakra. It is gold light, connected to the divine knowing of God, your connection to Source. This level is part of the celestial field, beyond space and time.

Well, we have learned a lot about perception. You and I will continue our momentum by going straight to meditation and energy hygiene, both so important to every individual.

Chapter 6:
Meditation and Energy Hygiene

"My soul is my guide."

Rumi

This part of Wisdom is so that while you grow, you may come from a place of clarity and experience the world from a place of Source. These suggestions are usually a daily practice.

Bija Meditation

The bija mantra was created at the beginning of time, before anything else was created. The bija mantras emerged as the first manifestation of creation; they are spiritual seed vehicles that take you back to Source. They are a vibration, and can only be felt as a pulse; they are not a word of any language. They have been used by the ancient Siddhas for over 2,500 years to attain enlightenment. They work on the physical, mental, and emotional level, including clearing of both individual karma and family karma. The techniques feed all the subtle bodies and all of the systems of the physical body. Each vital current is strengthened: the organs, emotions, etc., that are associated with that prana are also strengthened and healed, the light body is enhanced, and the ascension process accelerated. They are passed from teacher to student through a 5,000-year- old ceremony, sung in Sanskrit. This is not a religious ceremony.

Everyone who participates in TheoSophia's Wisdom School receives a heart bija mantra. This technique of meditation is not only a healing technique, it also releases your personal karma. Automatic transcendence of thought occurs in two to three minutes. The meditation is done twice a day for 20 minutes at a sitting, approximately eight hours apart. Maintaining this practice will offer you the ability to walk in your world in a calm, heart-centered state. This is a meditation where you do not have to quiet the mind. You allow your thoughts to work for you. It is done simply by sitting in a chair, calling forth the mantra to take you inside, letting it disappear, and letting your consciousness follow it. Other thoughts will begin to come into the mind. This is ok – these thoughts are coming up to release karma. You could have thoughts about your day, yesterday, or tomorrow; don't pay any attention to them. They are not important. Imagine you are in a movie theater and allow the thoughts to jump on a train to release them from your consciousness. The thoughts are your karma. Even if you were to have a profound experience, like Moses standing in front of you in your imagination, in this technique you will give it no credence, due to it being karma releasing. If this were a true message, it would return three different times in three different meditations. Just imagine it going on the train and let it go.

Bija mantras are God in motion. They guide you home, deep inside the sacred place within you. The use of these techniques reminds you of belonging, that which we all yearn for. This technique is like a diamond in the rough: simple beyond words, yet more valuable than anything in our human existence. This is one thing in the universe that is reliable, and it has been around since the beginning of time. If it were not valuable, it would have been lost long ago.

There are many benefits of Bija meditation, both physical and psychological. The physical benefits include stress relief, removing the cardiac stress from around the heart, releasing the lactic acid in the muscles, and many more. From the psychological point of view, there is IQ enhancement and emotional balance – all things considered, these have the capacity to change your life. You will begin to see life through the eyes of love, letting go of the illusion of our world, and breathing in the moment. This is a perfect scenario for your journey, and this is exactly why it is offered in this school. It is a perfect partner to support your growth.

A Refreshing Shower/ Clearing Energy Cords

I'm sure there have been times when you have been out to spiritual events for the day or shopping all day. Have you ever realized you feel tired afterwards? Ok, there is a very good reason for this. We just spent some time learning you are not only a human being, but also an energy and spiritual being. When you, or anyone, are around a lot of people, you can experience an energy drain. People are not always aware they are experiencing it, as I'm sure you are not, either. A few facts: Every time we touch another person, an energy cord attaches. Every time you think of someone, energy goes to that person, and it's the same when they think of you. By the time you return home, you are carrying a lot of energy with you that is not yours – not to mention the chemical substances in the air from perfume and such. So, if these additional energies are not addressed, the weight of the burden builds upon itself. For some people, it can even lower their immune system.

We are talking about vibration, also known as frequency. Each of us has an energy field called an aura, and each of us lives within that aura at a different frequency. The frequency depends on the state of your being: It could be high and moving very fast, or low and barely making a movement. There are a lot of components that affect this light quotient frequency, which is what it is called. In situations as I mentioned above, cords from other people attach to your chakra, which lowers the rate of vibration for that chakra, which then lowers the rate of the vibration of the level of the field out around the body. The result is that you are either tired, grumpy, sad, or whatever lower experience that all the other people were feeling. I understand it sounds very complicated. Let's talk about what to do.

First, when you get home from being out, take a shower if you feel not like yourself in any way. Once in the shower, run water from cool to warm, back and forth. This will help to clear the aura and balance the emotional field. Second, call forth Archangel Michael; he always stands to the right front of you to help you. He will come forth with his blue, flaming sword and release all cords from all chakras that are not of your truth. With your thoughts, think of each chakra, imagining

Archangel Michael releasing cords from your chakras, front and back. You will most likely feel a calmness coming over you. I know you will feel like you again.

The Violet Flame

In 1930, an Ascended Master called St. Germain brought forth the Violet Flame to the earth. The Violet Flame is an energy that, when called upon, comes from three feet below your feet, ten feet around you, and fifteen feet above you, and within the aura burns karma: past, present, and future. The Karmic Board, which consists of eight Ascended Masters, is assigned to daily weigh the balance of mankind's use of energy as it affects the spiritual ecosystem of the planet. It was decided that humanity needed help healing our karma. It is best to use the Violet Flame two or three times a day for a short period of time. Using the Violet Flame means that we no longer have to find the person we have karma with to work it out. Today, you can simply call in the Violet Flame from a heart space, allowing the Violet Flame to come to you.

The 14 Ray: The Clear Light of God

In TheoSophia's Wisdom School, I ask all my students to begin to use the 14 Ray – the clear light of God – whenever they are doing healing, on themselves or another person. The 14 Ray is crystal-clear energy that, as you develop, will become a flame of light that will have the capacity to turn light into matter and matter into light. As Albert Einstein said: $E = mc^2$. Once it becomes flame, it is called Mother Light. It is the highest light in the universe. Why would you use anything else?

Archangel Pyramids, Golden Pyramids

The Archangel Pyramids is a favorite protective practice of mine. It is done in the morning, and as often as you feel you need it. It will bring angels from below, from above, and all around you. This and all the other techniques I will talk about will build for you as you use them. You cannot give an angel the job to create it for you, you must be a participant. You will use your gift of perception to feel the angels and how they are affecting your energy field. The Golden Pyramid is for placing its energy around you, your home, state, America, the Earth, and the Universe. It also is very powerful.

Why Is Protection Important?

Let's get to the real question. There is a lot of negativity in the world today, despite how much all the light workers attempt to negate it. Unfortunately, it still exists. Darkness is drawn to the light. As you grow, you become a higher light. It is important to remain in clarity as you are doing your sessions and releasing your stuff, whatever it is. You can always call in the White Light of God to protect you. Most importantly, it is for you to create the habit of setting the energy around you. You have been living in this world not knowing this truth. This is for you to live life as a light being. Do the work, and it will protect you. Remember, in the beginning you may have to set your protection many times throughout the day. When you find yourself in an emotional situation, your energy vibration lowers, and all your protection dissipates.

Becoming the Observer

As you choose to become an observer in your life, you will begin to let go of judgment and criticism. Growth will come, and as it does, how you see the world will change. I invite you to begin to realize that every person you see is filled with the light of God. The degree of their knowing it can be from one to ten. From living in the human world, it is quite common for us to begin to identify ourselves with what has occurred from the time of our birth, until today. This is a huge error. You can only identify yourself today, in truth, when through healing you have learned about other experiences, other places, and other heights you have obtained. This will all be revealed to you in perfect timing, when you are ready to accept the truth. The gifts you are trying to understand most likely came from a life you had in another time or dimension, a time when you had perfect sight in the third eye, and you just don't remember. As you do the work and begin to find yourself, all things shall be revealed in perfect time.

Simply, at your next available moment, reset all your protection. You should get to where it doesn't take but a few minutes.

If you would like to receive the two protective meditations I mentioned above, simply e- mail me at: theosophiaswisdom@gmail.com And I will send them to you.

Some Case Studies on Energy Hygiene

1. A man named Tim, 44, was on his spiritual path. He was on a three-week meditation trip with a group of 14 people. During his process of meditating using the Holy Spirit mantra, he brought up memories of the years he was in the war. It was very intense, so I quickly had him go to his room and take a shower, running the water from cold to hot. It only took a few minutes for him to calm down, be able to talk through his memories with me, and let them go. It is a wonderful tool.

2. In school, many different things come up, and I will share one experience here, offering you the opportunity to learn. The students were given the techniques of the pyramids I mentioned above. A few weeks later, one of the students came to school, claiming it didn't work for her. I listened closely and asked her how she was doing it, and how often she was creating the pyramid. Her name is Nancy and she is 54. She stated she had busy mornings, so she gave the job to an angel, and was only thinking about doing it that one time. Well, immediately I found her problem. I explained to her that spiritual work needs you to show up for it to work. I understood being busy, that only means she has a scheduling issue. Perhaps it would help to go to bed earlier to have time to complete her spiritual work in the morning. In the beginning, you may have to do the protections many times a day; it does not take long. Also, it is a process of calling in an archangel, enjoying feeling the angel, and asking it to be there

in your field for you. Use your perception and sense the color. It will all help you to grow. All the spiritual work you are given to do addresses many things. All of it helps you to strengthen your abilities.

Case Studies on Bija Meditation

1. Scott, 41, went to a four-week meditation retreat in Thailand. He had a problem with his mother and wanted to release it. No matter what was going on in Scott's life, his mother would criticize him. So, he held his intention and meditated every day, asking for this to be released. For approximately 15 hours a day, he closed his eyes and allowed the thoughts to come into his mind. After he got home, a miracle had happened. His mother never criticized him again. Why did this shift happen? Scott's mother had simply been mirroring how Scott had felt about himself. Scott had set himself free from a life of never thinking he was good enough.

2. Lorraine 36, went on a 10-day retreat, meditating with the Bija mantras. She had two sisters. One sister was a shut-in and never went out of the house. Her other sister, she never saw. Lorraine meditated for the 10 days, and went home to find that her shut-in sister had moved out to a new place and was enjoying life again. Her other sister had contacted them to get together and re-connect. Family karma is an interesting thing. We never know what we hold inside, until it is gone and we are free.

Your experience of meditation will be a gentle and awakening process. It is a great support system that allows you to be calm and clear about your choices in life.

As we move forward, we are going to look at working with clients, and learn about techniques that you will be able to use on yourself and others.

Chapter 7:
Working with Clients

"Start by doing what's necessary; then do what's possible; and suddenly you are doing the impossible."

Francis of Assisi

The Art of Listening

Together, we have been moving toward your desire to help others. I feel that listening is one gift that is worth millions. Sure, we have all had opportunities to listen in our lives, but when you are working with another person's soul, it is time to tune in with respect, honoring the place they sit, and knowing their soul is sacred. It is very likely they are not aware of these three words: sacred, honor, and respect. I believe it is a part of our job to encourage, to support, and to embrace an individual while they are attempting to discover a greater love for themselves. Mind you, I do not mean to placate them at all. Sometimes the truth may be uncomfortable, yet necessary. Your awareness of when to be quiet and listen, or to speak and be heard is one of the greatest dances in your journey.

When you sit with a client and they start to share with you what they believe is going on, it is time for you to listen. Let's remember a few things: It is very rare for an individual to come in and know what is upsetting them. Their ego has tried to tell them what is going on. Usually individuals are in denial of the real reason. Some may not be ready to hear it, let alone experience it. When I say the word "listen," I am also saying to be gentle. I listen, while at the same time, I am feeling in my heart for what they aren't saying, and looking at their body language to understand how they are physically feeling. Often a question will come to mind. I have learned over the years to trust what comes, so I just ask them what I hear in my heart.

Usually it will bring on a mountain of tears. A door has been opened, and the work begins. In the next few chapters, we will look at techniques for you to use with your clients.

There are many parts of this you may naturally have within you. Feeling the call to help people, you more than likely already have a servant's heart. Within my own practice, I never forget I was once the person across from me.

Healing is an interesting thing. I remember a teacher once told me to contemplate how Jesus facilitated such profound healings. Back then, my response was because he was God's Son. Let me see if I can show you the error in my thinking. Jesus could heal due to his understanding about God, faith in God, truth, and the inner work he accomplished on his path. For instance, he wasn't only God's Son, he owned that he was the Son of God. He had faith that the love of God moved through him. Lastly, he knew how to hold thought so profoundly that if a man was blind, he would touch him knowing what the man's truth was: He could see. Transformation complete. If there is a goal, at least for me, it would be to be so clear, to have a faith so deep, and to have such a practice of thought that it would show as a miracle. I'm working on it. You can, too. All men were created in perfection. Life has occurred to have them forget the good, the strength, the love, and the inner beauty. As a healer, you can help them remember who they really are. It is through the art of listening.

Sacred, Honor, and Respect

Let's look a little deeper into those three words. Honor: Contemplate for a moment, how it would feel to honor yourself? It means to have high self-esteem and recognition. Respect: again we see the word esteem in the definition, along with a high regard. Sacred means having a connection to God or dedicated to a purpose of the servant's heart. All souls are sacred. They might not know it or feel it, but you and I can choose to see all beings as sacred, increasing the light and love in the world. Perhaps you can feel the vibration we are creating, even before we begin a healing. First, you feel these things within you, then bring them forward to offer to the client. We are going to work with energy. Even if we only talk, thoughts are energy. Remember the law: Energy follows thought.

Alignment: Getting Prepared to Offer Healing

First, we take a moment and ground ourselves into the earth. Remember to offer with the palms of your hands facing upward. When you begin to bring the energy up, ask your ego to move into alignment with your Higher Self and your Higher Self into alignment with your "I AM" Presence, which is your individualized presence of Mother Father God. Now you have brought yourself up into your highest light. You will find yourself breathing upward as you go. Next, we must do the same with your chakras. Start with the root chakra, scarlet red, imagine it spinning about six inches wide. Next, up to the second chakra and do the same. Go through all the chakras, just like this, to have an opened energy field. Send light through your Sushumna, connect your head, heart, and hands together. You are pretty much ready to go. When your client comes in, give them an information sheet to fill out. While they do so, you will with intention raise their alignment up with yours. It is all very focused, and always the same.

Transference

Transference is the misplacement of feelings and desires from childhood toward a new person. This often happens in healing work, when, for instance, if someone comes to you to work on family issues. First, I hope you had a wonderful mother, or have already worked on your mother issues. If there is a reason that you have not, I suggest not accepting this client. Refer them to someone else. You can only help those whose patterns you have already resolved yourself. This, again, is why you must be a participant in your own healing. If you are sitting with a client and your own stuff comes up, you will be helping no one. How do you know when your stuff is coming up? You will feel emotionally connected to the drama. Your ability to see beyond the problem is blocked.

There is another way transference can occur. Same client, you are clear on your mother issues. Your client feels so touched by your understanding that she sees you as her mother. This isn't a good situation, either, but it can go well if you have a good foundation within yourself and can support her in realizing you are not her mother. What I mean here is that your client will begin to show signs of anger at you in their session with you. Be strong in your intention, and it will become clear to your client that you are not her mother, and will allow her to release the anger.

I hope you continually see the importance of your own healing process. I have experienced both responses, and I have no problem referring someone. If I experience feelings from within myself, I cannot help the client. You must address these issues from your center, within your heart. It is your ego that wants to heal everyone.

Connecting to Your Healing Master and "I AM" Presence

There are two names of beings we have not yet talked about. When you decide to become a healer, or a facilitator of light, your energy field will change. Along with your Higher Self, there is a Healing Master that will come to you. From my experience, the Healing Master will stand to your right almost behind your shoulder, ready to whisper to you as information is needed. A Master is well-versed in healing and can help you with any problem you may have. It is a wonderful being for you to have with you and to learn from.

The "I AM" Presence is your individualized expression of God. It is connected to your heart, and usually hovers around 50 feet above you until you develop the ability to bring it down within you. In school, we learn how to sit for a healing as your "I AM" Presence. Understand your Presence responds to your pure thought. Your "I AM" Presence is not aware of your life upon Earth, it only knows God.

What Am I Responsible for as a Healer?

When you have begun on your spiritual path, it is important to know about responsibility.

There is only one thing you have to be responsible for: the clarity of your channel. This means you agree to work on remaining clear and surrendering to the light of God. If you have concerns about hurting someone while you are giving a healing, perhaps an old pattern from past lives is telling you that if you offer to help a person and they get worse afterwards, it will be your fault. It couldn't be further from the truth. We have no control as to how another soul responds to the gift of love we share with them. When I offer light to a person, their body takes that light and uses it where it wants to. I can only offer. So, relax, work on healing and discovering who you are. The rest will come easily.

Surrender

The back chakras of the sacral, solar plexus, heart, throat, and third eye are the chakras that resonate your will into the universe. These chakras hold the capacity to release the intention of the human being into the world; if their ego is strongly in charge, their will reacts – seeing the personality as the one who is important. Everything will be about the individual. When divinity has become part of the life stream, the chakras will react to the world through compassion, understanding, and service. Many people have a misunderstanding about surrendering. They think of times of war and of holding up the white flag. Giving up everything. This is not what surrendering is. The choice to surrender to God's will is simple: It is accepting this moment for what it is. This will bring calmness into every situation. You begin to know that every moment has a perfection to it. Even if you cannot see it at first, the realization will come. It may be best if I give you an example.

Let's imagine a man named Kyle. He is very much in the world, and values his place in it: how much money he makes, how he looks. He wants to be stylish, and have a great car. His concerns are all about himself. Most likely, he spends a lot of time feeling unhappy about his life. Let's look at another man, Sam. He holds a servant's heart. He cares a great deal about his family, and tends to put them first. He is a fireman, works for the city where he lives, and holds a great concern about the community. He embraces the fulfillment his outlook gives him. He lives each moment as it comes. His faith is deep, and he is committed to living in God's light.

Two different men; nothing wrong with either. We can see from the development of their back chakras how they were responding in the world from a different place. A person who connects to the Light of God, lives in surrender. It is being at peace, and fulfilled from the truth and knowledge they believe about God, knowing they are safe. So, take a breath and gently close your eyes and surrender. Let go of the chaos, the dinner tonight, the grocery shopping, the kid's homework, all of it. Try to be in peace. You may like the feeling. Accept the moment.

Case Study

Violet, 52, came to my school because she was looking for something to keep her busy. She had retired, apparently too early, and wanted to give something back to the world. When we got to learning techniques and working on each other in class, she would just cry. She said she couldn't do it. When others in the class looked at her, they would see an old monk sitting in her seat, crying. We worked on this issue in her healing sessions and had to release times when she had hurt people in her past lives. Sometimes the past lives came up even though she wasn't hurting anyone in her life today. Once released, the crying stopped and a great compassion came forward toward her clients. Again, it is all about doing the work. Heal thyself.

Certainly, you can begin to see the importance of experiencing your healing with a gifted person, allowing you to learn. Do the work and the rewards will flow like a waterfall for you. Next, we are going even deeper into the world of chakras.

Chapter 8:
Insight About Working with Chakras and Their Analysis

"Yesterday I was clever so I wanted to change the world. Today I am wise, so I am changing myself."

Rumi

Chakras, as they are known today, reach out through the aura of the human being for 352 levels. This journey is known as the Journey to the Monad, known as the divine spark that gives life to every human creature. This is a journey of climbing the ladder of evolution. We begin as human, embraced by the soul, known to be in a stage of development and evolution through multiple incarnational experiences, which extends over many lifetimes to the realization of the Mother Father God within. It is here we face our Monad, our higher consciousness that offers to the soul ideals, inspiration, and lessons toward perfections of chosen challenges in any one life. Development on this journey shifts to being about integrating your divinity at about level 33.

This will be a time of not only inner change, but of outward change. Beyond this, there are those people whom are becoming their Adam Kadmon body. The Adam Kadmon body is a replica of the light body, as you create it. The light body is the light you have received by expanding your consciousness, by the growth in consciousness from light given to an individual upon life accomplishments. During the development and growth, the chakras all transform into electrons of flaming light.

There are many levels of initiation on the journey of soul development. The soul has been you, since the beginning. It is the spirit part of you. When I began on my journey, I was driven to find what "soul" means. Every book I read, any class I went to, I wanted to know. The answer really came to me when I could see it. The body is of matter. It is of a slower particle spin than the soul part of you, which is your spirit.

I believe we have all lived many lives, and we take our issues and spiritual development from one life to the next. Most of the time, we are in a process of remembering who we have been, due to the veil of forgetting we pass through during our birthing process. We all have many soul families: individuals we have lived with in other lifetimes. Have you ever met someone and felt that you have known them before? There is no mistake – this is true. The soul part of us is constantly guiding us toward beings, places, and situations that will help us remember on our journey. It is also very possible you have had profound gifts in another life, and are just now beginning to remember them and feel the passion you once held when you used them. It is all wondrous to me. Perhaps it will be to you, also.

The word "chakra" is actually a Sanskrit term meaning "wheel of light." Chakras manage, support, and regulate the physical, emotional, mental, astral, and spiritual energies upon the Earth plane. The chakras are each connected to a specific dimension of the universe. They will each have a front and back chakra, except for the root and crown.

Working with Chakras

I find that working with chakras is like looking through the window – through the looking glass. After listening to a client, I access all my abilities to receive how I am able to help the individual. For example, the heart chakra can be very different inside. Depending on the level of development, the heart chakra is normally filled with a beautiful, emerald-green light flowing everywhere. There will be a large waterfall along the back wall, a river that runs through, and a huge beehive filled with the nectar of God. When the relationship with God is developed, there will be a beautiful beach connecting with the Ocean of God. Now, when self-love has not been existing for a while, the heart chakra will be dried up like the desert. There will be pain, sorrow, and grief present. Not to worry: All things are capable of transformation. With love, the Light of God, and perhaps some gentle understanding, things will move into wisdom.

Sometimes, the message I get will be to use the animal of the chakra. Let's go to the second chakra, which usually has something to do with the individual's sexuality. So, we will look inside to see what the power animal for the second chakra – the alligator – is doing. It is a representative of the action. For instance, if we see it lying on a beach and not moving, it tells us there is no sex life. If the alligator is trolling through the river, we know it is active. All these visions will help us resolve our client's problem.

At times, I will simply see a door or doorway. This says to me that there is a large fear preventing entrance into this chakra. Through conversation, I will discover the fear and will help the client move the energy.

When I look at the aura, sometimes in a certain area of the body, there will be no energy movement. I know this means the chakra is no longer connected to the Sushumna. It is not receiving any life force from the channel. Here, I imagine the lotus as a plant. I look to the roots of the plant and see that most likely it is not connected, so I replant it into the channel. Light pours in like a waterfall. We breathe together and continue.

The chakras will speak of how they are doing. This will develop your gift of perception as you work on feeling and seeing energy as well as understanding their message to you.

Working with light and matter – and observing them transforming – is certainly a magic to experience.

Transformational Properties of the Chakras

Let's continue our journey into understanding the chakras that make up your energetic self.

#1 Root Chakra

The root is the seat of physical vitality and the fundamental urge to survive. It regulates the systems that keep the body alive; it is where innocence thrives in the body. Upon development of this chakra, man becomes co-creator with God.

- Location: base of the spine
- Color: red
- Mantra: *Lam*
- Animal: elephant
- Qualities: manifestation, survival, grounding, stability, trust, self-preservation, and desire to be in the physical world
- Sense: smell
- Glands: adrenals
- Parts of body: legs, feet, bones, large intestine
- Gem: coral
- Planet: Mars
- Excessive spin: overly possessive; fearful parent
- Deficient: homeless, ungrounded, and victim energy

#2 Sacral Chakra

This chakra is where you hold relationships that are in flux. The front is the emotional chakra, while the back of this chakra is where the quality of your sexuality lies, along with perception of finances. A shift in consciousness occurs when these issues are healed and the chakra becomes a creative center of multiple colors to bring in ideas and movement. The goal is intimacy, within the self.

- Location: slightly below the navel
- Color: orange
- Mantra: *Vam*
- Animal: alligator

- Qualities: relationships, sexuality, empathy, pleasure, well-being, connection, delight, emotions, feelings, polarity, and change
- Sense: taste
- Glands: testicles, reproductive organs
- Parts of body: lower abdomen, kidney, bladder
- Gem: amethyst
- Planet: Mercury
- Excessive spin: manipulative, controlling, lustful, addictive
- Deficient: co-dependent, martyr, submissive, doesn't feel anything

#3 Solar Plexus

Your creativity is fueled by your will. This is the home of the soul. Upon a journey within, you will discover your soul temple.

- Location: below the rib cage
- Color: yellow
- Mantra: *Ram*
- Animal: ram
- Qualities: joy, motivation, self-esteem, transformation, identifications, mastery, willpower over own light, power in relationship with others, vitality, energy, standing steady in self, desire to express individuality
- Sense: sight, intuition
- Gland: pancreas
- Parts of body: stomach, liver, and gallbladder
- Gem: emerald
- Planet: Jupiter
- Excessive spin: egotistical, self-absorbed, ambitious, self-driven warrior, desire to take control

- Deficient: poor self-worth, greed, fear, hate, selfishness, criticism, ulcers, sensitive servant, feels disliked, martyr, needing to do all the time.

#4 Heart Chakra

When front and back heart chakras are working together, we find our truth and love for all aspects of ourselves and come from a place of safety. This enables us to surrender to the Divine will. This is the bridge connecting the lower and higher energies of our being.

- Location: center of chest
- Color: emerald
- Mantra: *Yum*
- Animal: dove, black panther
- Qualities: compassion, love, open-hearted, forgiving, peaceful, joyful, ability to go after what we want, desire for self-acceptance, balance, emotion, harmony, place of integration
- Sense: touch
- Glands: thymus
- Parts of body: heart, liver, lungs, blood circulation
- Gem: ruby
- Planet: Venus
- Excessive spin: inappropriate emotional expression, poor emotional boundaries
- Deficient: ruthless, no heart, can't feel emotions, repression of love, emotional instability, seeking to make world safe by controlling others

#5 Throat Chakra

- Location: throat
- Color: light to dark blue

- Mantra: *Hum*
- Animal: deer
- Qualities: communication, creativity, sound, intuition, synthesis, giving and receiving, self-expression, desire to speak and hear the truth
- Sense: hearing
- Gland: thyroid
- Parts of body: throat, upper lungs, arms, digestive track
- Gem: sapphire
- Planet: Saturn
- Excessive spin: willful, controlling, judgmental, hurtful
- Deficient: lacking faith, unable to creatively express, silent child, knowledge used unwisely, ignorance, fear of failure, sees self as a victim, lack of confidence

#6 Third Eye

This is the chakra of forgiveness and compassion. The back chakra is known as the zeal point, the chakra of manifestation. It is through the front chakra the dream is visualized, and the back manifests the dream. It is very important that both are open and functional.

- Location: forehead
- Color: indigo
- Mantra: *Aum*
- Animal: owl
- Qualities: light, knowingness, intuition, perception, self-mastery, wisdom, imagination, vision, clairvoyance, seat of creativity, insight, concentration, mind over matter
- Sense: sight, vision
- Gland: pituitary

- Parts of body: spine, lower brain
- Gem : diamond
- Planet: Sun
- Excessive spin: overly intellectual, overly analytical
- Deficient: unclear thought, deluded, hopelessness, escaping from reality into head trips, misuse of psychic powers, scatter-brained, lack of direction, headaches

#7 Crown

This chakra represents the highest level of consciousness and enlightenment. It is the connective center to spirit. Balance of this chakra will tell you that you are beginning to understand you are a spiritual being living a human existence.

- Location: top of the head
- Color: pink
- Mantra: *Ah*
- Animal: eagle
- Sense: knowingness
- Parts of body: upper brain and right eye
- Planet: Pluto
- Deficient: no spiritual inspiration or aspiration

The Petal Work

This is a technique that is all about the chakras. Let's check it out here.

I discovered that all the chakras individually needed qualities of all the other chakras within them to function. For instance, imagine if the heart chakra wasn't rooted, or the root had no heart. This can be a problem. I was shown how to resolve this issue. We can do it simply by using energetic beads. Imagine that each chakra has a bowl of beads of their color and action within them. So, when I go and I see the heart needs to be rooted and needs some creative energy, I will have my client go down their channel to the root and place a red bead from the root into the backpack they have on their back. I have them stop at the second chakra and get an orange bead, full of creativity, and put it into the backpack, and then move up the inner channel to the heart and release the beads into the energy. The heart will receive and burst into new light. It is quite powerful.

In the same way, if the root had no heart, you would travel up the inner channel and take an emerald green bead from heart, place it in your backpack, and take it down the channel and offer it to the root. An explosion of compassion would occur, allowing your root chakra to perceive the world differently and feel a different safety. Perhaps you can see what I mean. There are other levels of this work that are just as captivating.

We will continue our journey to observe some other techniques to help resolve issues.

This is where the magic takes a higher turn.

Chapter 9:
How and Why Healing Techniques Change Lives

"The moment you accept the troubles you've been given, the door will open."

Rumi

Subconscious Release Technique

I will begin with giving you the definition of subconscious mind. It relates to thoughts and feelings that exist in the mind and influence your behavior although you are not aware of them. This part of the mind notices and remembers information on the fringe of consciousness and contains material of which it is possible to become aware.

The important part of this definition is that thoughts and feelings can influence your behavior although you are not aware of them. None of us know what really exists in our subconscious mind. This means you, too. This work has proven so powerful to release patterns that are held in the subconscious mind. Imagine for a moment that you are at work, and an unruly person comes into your business, wanting to know something about your town. You find yourself repeating the words, getting frustrated. After he leaves, you stop to contemplate: What just happened?

Well, I can only guess that somewhere in your subconscious mind, there is a memory of feeling attacked or bullied by a man, and those thoughts and feelings are being triggered and have resurfaced. Or maybe you were feeling unheard. We call whatever pattern that emerges a tape – a tape that is held within your subconscious either waiting to be triggered again or to be released. Somewhere deep inside, there is a core issue, and while it may take many releases of this technique to reach the core and set it free, it will work. I find this works best on third- dimensional issues.

So now the how. I can sense you are becoming inquisitive. Without going into all the details, I will tell you. After supporting the client in getting into a calm receptive state, we release the pattern by using affirmations, visualizations, sound, and energetic processes that specifically free the tape we are working on. Slowly, as we work together and release various patterns, the client begins to change, and many times the client's family begins to change.

Here is a list of possible blocks in the subconscious mind:

- criticism, condemnation
- disorder, confusion
- trespassing, the need to dominate
- fear of exposure, embarrassment, shame
- hatred, anger, resentment
- worry, anxiety
- fear of self-expression
- jealousy, covetousness, competition
- non-resistance
- abundance, unlimited good
- freedom, self-authority, release
- joy
- Qualities: spirit, Shiva, consciousness, unification of colors, intelligence, bliss of Divine wisdom and Divine knowing
- Gland: pineal
- Gem: pearl

- Excessive spin: egomaniac, lack of inspiration, confusion, hesitation to serve, senility, depression
- fight or flight
- poverty, lack
- bondage, possession
- pride, conceit
- sorrow for self; poor me
- self-repression
- guilt
- fatigue, illness, old age
- blaming others for our problems

Here are thoughts that dissolve blocks:

- non-judgment
- order, clarity
- permissiveness, respect for individuality
- honesty, sincerity, naturalness
- praise
- love, forgiveness
- life, light, true self-expression
- self-confidence, faith in inner revelation
- peace, poise
- self-acceptance, self-forgiveness
- perfect life, unlimited energy
- claiming our own good
- acknowledgment of self as cause for our experience

Inner Children Healing

This technique was spawned out of the subconscious work. Did you know that when you were a child, every time you could not understand, comprehend, or handle your emotions in a situation, you would hold your breath? At that time, a part of your consciousness separated and has held that same misperception within your subconscious, until you find it and embrace it with your love. Often, if we look at behavior, we will notice adults acting like a child, a teenager, or some version of a younger self. This work is very profound.

As you are listening to your client, you will hear that it is a child talking, perhaps with attitude. I will try to give you an idea of how this technique works. First, there is a process of finding the inner children – they are usually hanging out within a chakra. We call in a team of 20 angels to help move them out of the chakra. We then go through a process of healing the inner children by using affirmations, visuals, sound, or energy. They will transform and become light. The adult will hold one child to be representative of them all, in a rocking chair, allowing six months of time to pass. The adult being becomes the new mom, one who will never leave, offering love and comfort. When the process becomes complete, all the inner children of this patterning will be taken into a resort inside the heart to continue to grow, having everything they could possibly want. For 21 days, the adult will return to the resort in the heart to confirm to the inner children that they can begin to trust the adult and feel the comfort that they are there. This technique begins to rebuild the relationship within the self. A greater self-love will begin to be experienced.

Each pattern could hold from a few to hundreds of inner children. It seems to depend on how influential the children are to take over the life. You will find this to be a great process to help those who are looking to love themselves more.

The Judge and the Critic

Have you ever had a nagging voice in your head criticizing you and judging you? It's essentially the same principal as the Subconscious

Technique. Realize that the voice that sounds like a judge in your head is some part of your subconscious, and you've given it a job. Similarly, when communicating with a client, you will be able to determine what job the judge is doing for him. What you are going to do is give this energy known as the judge a pink slip and give it a new job.

I will explain: Perhaps the judging thought is about making your client feel like he is not good enough. This voice has belittled him all his life. Have your client imagine sitting at a desk and writing out a pink slip, thanking the judge for all he has done, but telling him that he is fired. Next, we need a positive new job. The energy of the judge is a part of your client, so we cannot let it go, but we can change it to a positive. We are going to tell your client to give the judge the pink slip and breathe deeply three times. The energy of the judge will have dissipated. Now ask your client to breathe deeply three times with the positive thought – for this example, let's use "I am good enough" – allowing the energy to become an angel. Now your client has an angel to be with him, reminding him that he is good enough.

If the voice in your head is a critic, it will sound a little more like a continual whine.

Imagine a bubble around the voice and give it a pop with a pin – in your imagination of course. It will immediately disappear.

Holographic Healing

Holographic Healing is a technique that expands simply working with the chakras on the body. I was shown that there is a field of chakras like the Internet, both major and minor chakras, above the body. For a moment, contemplate your heart chakra on your chest. Now imagine 351 more chakras in a line above it.

I can remember my first thought was, "How do you reach all of them?" But as I worked on it, all my questions were answered. This technique is done only on the right arm. All seven chakras are placed along the arm. The communicating chakra is the throat, of course. It will give you the information very expertly. First, you will offer the client light to fill the field. As you do this, you will receive information from the throat chakra. Even if the client comes with a specific issue, there is always more information coming from the body elemental. For more on this, see the case study on Betty at the end of this chapter.

Voice Healing

Let's discuss how you can begin to support yourself and your energy field by starting to use your voice. First, I want you to start singing. Don't give a thought to how your voice sounds, you want to give it permission to give sound. Believe me, after doing this for a while, your voice will change. Don't sing so much that your throat hurts, but every day, do your best to let your voice sing out. If it does strain your vocal cords a bit, you can ask your doctor if it is ok to use slippery elm – an herb– to sooth your throat. You can then begin to sing the do re me scale. You may be beginning to wonder, what is my voice going to do for me? Well, let me explain.

Sound is going to become the way of healing in the future. Heart healing will follow closely. Just as technology has taken over electronics, sound will become the most accessible and most profoundly accurate healing method. It is about the vibration and the frequency. Remember, I said earlier that evolving is all about raising your light quotient? This is increasing the particle spin of your energy field.

We all have a favorite song. Mine is *Somewhere over the Rainbow*. Years ago, I sang this in the car when I was driving, since I had no radio. Little did I know this was creating a strength, new octaves, and a whole new vibration in my voice. The first type of healing I invite you to do is on yourself. You will begin by toning your own chakras. Yes, I know, a lot is out there about toning the chakras. We are laying the groundwork to heal, with this voice in training. I have had students who were barely able to sing a note eventually create beautiful sounds of healing.

Everybody is different. You could get a pitch pipe, or perhaps pull up notes on your iPhone. Here are the notes and sounds for the chakras:

- Root: C, oh
- Sacral: D, oo

- Solar plexus: E, ah
- Heart: F, ay
- Crown: B, sing

The pitch is very low in the root chakra, and continues to get higher as you move up your chakras. When you arrive eventually at your crown, make the sound of the note while you are saying the word "sing." Take note to observe what you are feeling within your body. Increase your sense perception. You are doing great. This will begin to become really easy, yet always sit in consciousness asking to understand more, and ask, "Please show me." This is practicing being in surrender.

Case Study: Holographic Healing

Betty 54, had difficulty going to the bathroom on her own. She had taken laxatives for many years. She had worked with doctors and naturopaths, but nothing had helped. She came to see me. It came to me to do the Holographic technique on her, so I could see what was really going on. The information from her body elemental was very informative. The situation was a result of karma from a long, long time ago. Her intestines had been ripped out of her. She had no control over the situation; it was a punishment of some sort. I was informed I would have to go back to a chakra that held the vibration of a healthy colon and intestine before whatever had been experienced was done. As I placed my hand over the root chakra on the arm, I immediately began to move up the line of chakras. All I saw were sick-looking ones that were very weak, they had no color. I kept going. Around the 180th chakra, everything seemed worse. I eventually moved beyond the agony to a well-balanced, lively looking chakra: number 215. As I held this chakra in pause, I traveled down to the one in her physical body and released it. In that moment, all the chakras from 1 to 214^{h} dissipated. I brought the healthy chakra down and connected it into the Sushumna. The energy began to move like a normal root chakra would. Betty mentioned that she could feel energy moving. We talked for a while, letting the body settle, while I balanced the rest of her field. She left to go home and we felt optimistic. Remember this was done on an energetic level. The healing took much longer than it sounds in this case study. Betty called me two days later. She had experienced a bowel movement on her own, and she felt great. The technique worked. God always says to me, "TheoSophia, the work always works!"

Case Study: Subconscious Release

A gentleman named John, 67, came to see me. He had a large, eggplant-sized, cancerous tumor on his left side of his head. He had tried everything, and wanted to see if I could help. We sat together and I began to sense that I was constantly looking at his hands. I asked him what he did for a living. Was it something with his hands? He replied that yes, he had been a bouncer in a bar all his life.

You may not know, but the hands are a similar energy to the head. The knuckles are the eyes. He had literally spent his life grabbing and hitting people with his hands. He told me from my asking him about his temperament that he had been angry all his life. I explained the knuckles on his hands. They were where the cancer had come from. We began sessions every week doing the subconscious work, releasing various levels of anger from within him. I gave him visualizations to do. He went to have tests done often to see if things changed. Before we knew it, he had gone into remission.

This has been quite a chapter. The work can bring so much change into a person's life. I hope you are getting as excited as I am for you. I hope you can see there is so much, through your gifts, you can offer to another person. Perhaps you can begin to see why I love what I do.

Chapter 10:
How to Handle the Obstacles

"You never fail until you stop trying."

Albert Einstein

I have shared with you how I solved the problem of having gifts, not knowing what to do with then, and wanting very much to develop them. For me, it became a passion. I still experience that passion growing inside me every day. Here I am, writing this book to you, something I had never done. I have seen many individuals start this path, as well as some of the things that come up for them. First, I think it is important to remind you that all troubles are transformable into a positive. It is all about perception.

You may find that your biggest obstacle is yourself. When you are on the path of awakening, the one thing you can count on is change. We all have fears, an ego, judges, and critics in the subconscious. It's true that others could bring these things up for us, but in the end, we must step back and realize that the fear is coming from within us. My study of consciousness has revealed to me that fear is the catalyst that helps us move forward.

When my daughter was in her early teens, I was trying to help her let go of a fear. She looked up at me with her beautiful green eyes and said, "Mommy, I got it, the big old dragon roared at me, and I just kissed it and it became a lamb." Sometime the simplest thing is the greatest option. God is simple. You and I, being human, tend to put things into a turmoil and then try to figure it out. What I am really saying is that if any of these things come up, look them straight in the eye. See if you can see beyond the fear. There, you will find a door – a door to a whole new adventure about you. This journey is yours and for those you choose to share it with.

One of my students, Jane, is a woman who has chosen to be on her path. She has a degree in psychology and has never used it. She chose to study with me in the Wisdom School and loved it. Her issue was that she was easily distracted. She would decide to leave the school, and then, within a short amount of time, she would miss the light and the work, I would get the call, and back she came. When her leaving and returning became an interference with the class, I suggested she do private mentoring so she could address the distraction issues in her session work. This is what she chose to do. I'm not saying I gave her permission to do what she wanted; she realized through our work that her distractions affected her life in many ways. She is doing better today and feeling less chaos.

Sometimes, the unspoken requirement of doing your inner work to grow can be challenging for individuals. When you are awakening, you must realize there is more to you than you are aware of right now. It has been spoken; we have always been enlightened, and our journey is about remembering it. I agree with this thinking. The more I grow and release places inside me that are tight and dark, the more blessings from God that I receive.

What is it like to try to undertake this journey on your own? Understand there is a subconscious part of you going on that journey with you: your ego. Its plan is not for you to grow in light, become empowered, or to change. It wants you to believe you need it – the ego – to grow. There is no way, in my opinion, that you will ever be able to see deeply enough into your own core issues to create the light you want to become.

But with help, with a mentor to help you grow, you can focus on the chakras and the issues you need to attend to. Things will move quickly when you are ready. Do the work, and all will evolve.

Chapter 11:
Embrace the Solution

"Imagination is everything. It is the preview of coming attractions."

Rumi

My wish for you is to live all your heart yearns for – becoming willing to go beyond the walls you have placed for yourself. Shine your heart, and those walls will look like a window – I encourage you to walk through it. Find a teacher and get excited about the journey before you. You have been on this journey for thousands of years, and there is a lot of discovery you have left for yourself to embrace. The healing never ends.

We have gone down an exciting road together. Talking about wisdom, magic, heart, and you. Learning about personal development and perception. All of this will support you in taking action and, in the end, unveiling your gifts. We then looked at meditation and energy hygiene, a great way to maintain a state of calm and clarity within your field. We ventured into observing how powerful working with clients can be. Once you develop your gifts, this could be you. Lastly, we learned all about the chakras: how they can transform your life and the various modalities that can bring release to yourself and others.

What do you do next? My suggestion is to remember why you decided to read this book. Correct me if I am wrong. You desired help to develop your gifts and to know how to use them. It's time for a good teacher or mentor to learn from. My wish is that you develop your gifts, and help other people while doing the work you love. Please keep in touch. Let me know your successes!

May God bless you. I am here for you.

Acknowledgments

There are many people I would like to acknowledge for their love and support.

To my husband, Douglas. Since the day we met 23 years ago in Thailand, he has been my rock, my love, and my biggest cheerleader. Our journey together has been an adventure and truly miraculous. He is truly a teddy bear.

To my best friend, Carol. Without her endearing friendship, this book would never have begun. We, too, have traveled on my adventures, within and without.

To my loving daughter, Heather, who gave me the breath of life each day when she said, "Type more, keep typing." She is an endearing soul, and knew her Momma would make it.

To my sweet Angel, Chance, who brings me JOY.

To the "girls" in Wisdom School: I'm so proud of how you have become so effortless in embracing your ups and downs.

To Donna, who would always say, "Someday you will be a great healer."

To Claudia for endless love during my deepest growth. We embraced my fears together.

You taught me how to be a good mentor and teacher.

To Bob, who touched the Buddhic part of me and allowed her to soar.

To Angela Lauria, for holding space for the writer within me to share her voice. I am eternally grateful.

To the ladies in the Idea to Done cohort, who kept me on my toes. You always seemed two steps ahead of me. Thank you.

To my inner teachers and angels, who are with me always, whose love, support, and wisdom have helped me become who I am today. I am honored.

The most special acknowledgment is to my parents, who are in heaven with God. My mother was truly the sweetest mother there ever was. My father could be a little cantankerous, but I so loved him anyway.

Lastly, to my Mother Father God. There are no words to say how I feel. You are alive within every cell of my being. I surrender.

About the Author

TheoSophia Rose is a spiritual mentor, guide, teacher, and a natural healer. Her personal studies have taken her from the mountains of Shasta to the caves of Thailand. Her heart guided her to becoming an initiator of Bija Meditation Techniques. She has traveled all over the country to offer individuals the heart mantra to help open the hearts of all souls. There have been many locations of her Healing School, all over the country from east to west. At this time, she has two schools ongoing: TheoSophia's Wisdom School and a Master Intensive Training. Her connection to the angelic realm is evident when she plays her nine alchemy crystal bowls with the angels. Upon hearing them, people say their bodies vibrate. Most people, upon hearing her speak from the heart, feel the vibration of love and her deep compassion. Her vision is crystal clear and unrestricted; her singing voice is transformative in the setting of a healing. When she works on the phone, she is often asked what instrument she is playing!

She is the founder of Illuminations of Light, Inc., 501c3, and her doctorate of philosophy is in Conscious Studies. She is the creator of Holographic Healing, The Petal Work, Subconscious Release Healing Modalities, and The Spiral Technique, which releases patterns at root cause. She is the author of *Timeless Wisdoms of Prosperity* and *TheoSophia's Wisdom School* and has appeared on various TV shows and radio stations across the country.

Her purpose stands steady, to help open the hearts of all souls and be a mentor to those who are working on their light path (ascension). Her unique work with groups and individuals helps to elevate planetary awareness and trigger super-consciousness within the masses. We are living in a time of great change; may you have the opportunity to walk your path with her.

Love is her guiding light.

Website: www.theosophiarose.com

Email: theosophiaswisdom@gmail.com

Facebook: TheoSophia Rose

Thank You

I would like to thank you for the time you have spent with me. I have a great fulfillment within my heart. I'm proud of you for getting to the end of this book, creating a new opportunity for your life. Willingness is needed to continue. I believe you have shown your commitment to becoming the light you are. Go forth and conquer. Conquer those parts of you that aren't aware of how truly beautiful you are. Your soul will radiate the light of your heart to the world. You must simply surrender to allow it all to come to be.

I would like to continue our discussion on this journey. I hope the work and the possibilities have inspired you to take the next step. If you would like more information about TheoSophia's Wisdom School, or just to stay in touch, or simply have a question, email me at theosophiaswisdom@gmail.com

I look forward to hearing from you.

www.ingramcontent.com/pod-product-compliance
Lightning Source LLC
LaVergne TN
LVHW041630070526
838199LV00052B/3302